Unveiling Dissent: Understanding the Critics of the United States

Table of Contents

Introduction: "Unveiling Dissent: Understanding the Critics of the United States"

The United States, a nation born from the aspirations of freedom and democracy, has evolved into a global powerhouse with a profound impact on the world stage. From the sprawling urban landscapes of New York City to the vast plains of the Midwest, the United States stands as a symbol of prosperity, innovation, and cultural diversity. Its journey from a fledgling colony to a superpower has been marked by triumphs, challenges, and a complex relationship with the international community.

In the 21st century, the United States finds itself at the forefront of global affairs, influencing economic policies, shaping geopolitical landscapes, and exporting its cultural products to every corner of the world. As the leader of the free world, the U.S. has been a beacon of hope for many, embodying the ideals of liberty, democracy, and the pursuit of happiness. However, alongside admiration, the United States has also garnered criticism and, at times, hostility from various quarters.

To embark on a journey of understanding the critics of the United States, we must first grasp the nation's global standing. The U.S. has undeniably been a force for progress, contributing to technological advancements, scientific breakthroughs, and cultural exports that have resonated globally. Its economic prowess has propelled the world forward, and the American dream has been a magnet for individuals seeking opportunities and a better life.

At the same time, the United States' global standing is a tale of contradictions and complexities. For every ally it has gained, there are critics who question its motives and actions. This book seeks to delve into the reasons behind the criticism, exploring the nuanced landscape of international relations and the myriad factors that have contributed to dissent.

A Superpower's Ascent: From Isolation to Global Dominance

The journey of the United States from an isolated colony to a global superpower is a testament to its resilience and adaptability. The late 18th century saw the birth of a nation as the thirteen colonies declared independence from British rule. The subsequent decades were marked by westward expansion, industrialization, and the consolidation of a diverse population.

By the mid-20th century, the United States emerged victorious from the ravages of World War II, marking the beginning of its ascent to global dominance. The post-war era saw the U.S. at the forefront of rebuilding war-torn nations through the Marshall Plan, establishing itself as a champion of democracy in the face of the rising Cold War tensions.

The Cold War Era: Ideological Struggles and Global Influence

The Cold War, a geopolitical struggle between the United States and the Soviet Union, defined much of the mid-20th century.

As the two superpowers engaged in ideological battles and proxy conflicts, the U.S. asserted its influence through economic aid, military alliances, and the promotion of democratic values.

The collapse of the Soviet Union in 1991 left the United States as the sole superpower, marking the beginning of a unipolar world order. With this newfound status came increased responsibilities and expectations, as the world looked to the U.S. for leadership in addressing global challenges.

Economic Powerhouse: The American Dream and Globalization

Central to the United States' global standing is its economic might. The American Dream, a concept rooted in the belief that anyone can achieve success through hard work, has attracted millions of immigrants seeking a better life. The U.S. became an economic powerhouse, fostering innovation, technological advancement, and unparalleled economic growth.

The end of the 20th century witnessed the acceleration of globalization, with the U.S. playing a pivotal role in shaping international trade and finance. The dollar became the world's primary reserve currency, and American corporations exerted influence on a global scale. However, this economic dominance has not been without consequences, as critics question the fairness of trade practices and the widening gap between the rich and the poor.

Cultural Hegemony: Hollywood, Technology, and Soft Power

Beyond economic and political influence, the United States has asserted itself culturally, exporting its values and way of life through the media and technology. Hollywood, with its iconic films and entertainment industry, has been a powerful tool for shaping perceptions worldwide. American technology companies, from Silicon Valley giants to social media platforms, have become synonymous with innovation and connectivity.

While the spread of American culture has been embraced by many, it has also sparked resistance and concerns about cultural imperialism. Critics argue that the dominance of American narratives in global media undermines local cultures and traditions, contributing to a homogenized global culture.

Challenges and Controversies: Navigating a Complex Landscape

As the United States solidified its position as a global superpower, it faced an array of challenges and controversies. Military interventions, perceived arrogance in foreign policy decisions, and instances of cultural insensitivity have fueled criticism from various quarters. The complexities of navigating a unipolar world have led to strained relations with nations that view U.S. actions with skepticism.

This book seeks to unravel the layers of dissent surrounding the United States, acknowledging its achievements while critically examining the factors that have generated animosity. In the chapters that follow, we will explore the historical context, political disagreements, economic disparities, cultural clashes, and the intricacies of power dynamics that contribute to the complex tapestry of international relations. By understanding the perspectives of those who criticize the United States, we aim to foster a more nuanced and informed dialogue about the challenges and opportunities that lie ahead in the interconnected world we share.

Purpose of the Book: Unveiling Dissent

The purpose of "Unveiling Dissent: Understanding the Critics of the United States" is to embark on a comprehensive exploration of the multifaceted reasons behind the criticism and hostility directed towards the United States on the global stage. This book aims to unravel the complex tapestry of international relations, shedding light on the diverse perspectives that contribute to dissent.

In a world interconnected by politics, economics, culture, and ideology, the United States, as a global superpower, has garnered both admiration and criticism. While many nations look to the U.S. as a symbol of freedom, democracy, and progress, others harbor reservations and animosity. The purpose of this book is to delve into the underlying factors that have fueled dissent, recognizing that understanding these perspectives is crucial for fostering meaningful dialogue and bridging gaps in a globalized world.

Key Objectives:

Historical Understanding: Explore the historical events and dynamics that have shaped the perceptions of nations critical of the United States. By tracing the roots of dissent, the book aims to provide context for contemporary criticisms and reveal the historical nuances that influence international relations.

Political Analysis: Examine the political motivations behind anti-American sentiment. Whether rooted in disagreements over international policies, alliances, or the exercise of diplomatic power, this book seeks to uncover the political dimensions that contribute to the strained relations between the U.S. and its critics.

Economic Perspectives: Investigate the economic factors that have led to criticism of the United States. From trade practices to economic disparities, the book aims to dissect the global economic impact of the U.S. and how these factors contribute to hostility from certain quarters.

Cultural and Ideological Insights: Delve into the cultural clashes and ideological differences that underpin criticism of the U.S. By exploring how American values, cultural exports, and the global influence of media shape perceptions, the book seeks to unravel the complexities of cultural dynamics in international relations.

Military Interventions and Global Stability: Address the impact of U.S. military interventions on global stability and sovereignty concerns. The book aims to analyze instances of military involvement and how they contribute to the perception of the United States as a global enforcer, both for good and ill.

Perceptions of Arrogance: Investigate how the U.S. is perceived as arrogant or hegemonic in its approach to global affairs. By examining unilateral decision-making and a perceived disregard for international opinions, the book seeks to uncover the roots of the critique of American foreign policy.

Global Power Dynamics: Explore the fear or resentment stemming from the U.S. as a global superpower and how power dynamics influence international relationships. The book aims to dissect the challenges and opportunities that arise from the unequal distribution of global power.

Religious and Social Dimensions: Examine how religious and social differences contribute to anti-American sentiments. By addressing cultural clashes related to values and beliefs, the book aims to uncover the social dimensions that influence perceptions of the United States.

Media Influence and Propaganda: Investigate how media portrayal shapes perceptions of the U.S. and the role of propaganda in influencing anti-American sentiment. The book aims to dissect the impact of media narratives on the formation of opinions about the United States.

Misunderstandings and Stereotypes: Address common misconceptions and stereotypes about the United States. By fostering a nuanced understanding, the book seeks to bridge cultural gaps and dispel myths that contribute to negative perceptions.

Through a balanced and in-depth exploration of these key dimensions, "Unveiling Dissent" aspires to contribute to a more nuanced and informed dialogue about the complex relationship between the United States and its global critics. By understanding the reasons behind the criticism and hostility, the book seeks to foster a deeper appreciation for the challenges and opportunities inherent in the evolving landscape of international relations.

Chapter 1: Historical Context

In the annals of global history, the United States emerges as a nation with a narrative woven through the threads of triumphs, struggles, and controversies. To understand the contemporary criticism directed at the United States, it is imperative to embark on a journey through its historical landscape. This chapter delves into pivotal historical events that have left an indelible mark on the nation, contributing to the negative perceptions that persist in certain quarters.

Colonial History: Seeds of Dissent

The origins of the United States are rooted in its colonial history, marked by the arrival of European settlers seeking religious freedom, economic opportunities, and a new way of life. However, the interaction between settlers and indigenous peoples laid the foundation for a legacy of displacement, violence, and cultural clashes. As we explore this historical period, we will unravel how the seeds of dissent were sown during the colonization era, influencing the perceptions of those who would later become critics of the United States.

The early chapters of American history are marked by the arrival of European settlers who sought to build a new life in the New World. While the colonial era laid the groundwork for the formation of the United States, it was not without significant conflict and tension, particularly with indigenous populations. The interaction between settlers and Native American tribes often resulted in displacement, violence, and cultural clashes.

Plymouth Colony: The establishment of Plymouth Colony in 1620 by English Pilgrims led to complex interactions with the Wampanoag tribe. Initial cooperation gave way to conflicts over land, resources, and cultural differences.

Expansion westward: As the U.S. expanded westward, conflicts with Native American nations intensified. The Trail of Tears, in the 1830s, saw the forced removal of Cherokee and other tribes from their ancestral lands.

Wars and Conflicts: Forging a Nation, Forging Hostility

The United States' journey to independence was fraught with wars and conflicts, each leaving an indelible imprint on the nation's identity. The Revolutionary War, the War of 1812, and the Civil War shaped the contours of the American landscape, but they also engendered animosity both internally and externally. This section will scrutinize how these conflicts, while defining the nation, may have contributed to negative perceptions among those who witnessed or experienced the impact of these wars.

The American Revolutionary War (1775-1783) was a pivotal moment in history, as thirteen colonies sought independence from British rule. While the war forged a new nation, it also left scars and fueled internal divisions. The War of 1812 and the Civil War further shaped the nation's identity but contributed to animosity both domestically and internationally.

Examples:

Revolutionary War: The conflict with Britain not only led to the birth of the United States but also strained relations with European powers, particularly Britain and France, as they navigated the complexities of post-war diplomacy.

War of 1812: Tensions with Britain persisted, leading to the War of 1812. The burning of Washington, D.C., by British forces, and issues such as impressment of American sailors, further strained relations.

Civil War: The Civil War (1861-1865) not only tested the unity of the nation but also had international repercussions. European nations, including Britain and France, closely watched the conflict and shaped their policies based on their perceptions of the U.S.

Interventions Abroad: From Idealism to Controversy

As the United States transitioned from an isolated nation to a global superpower, its interventions abroad became a defining feature of its foreign policy. From the Spanish-American War to involvement in conflicts across the globe, this section will explore how U.S. interventions, driven by a mix of idealism, strategic interests, and geopolitical considerations, have shaped international perceptions. The consequences of military interventions will be examined, shedding light on the complexities of projecting power beyond national borders.

As the United States emerged as a global power, its interventions abroad became a defining aspect of its foreign policy. While some interventions were motivated by idealistic goals, such as spreading democracy, others were driven by strategic interests, leading to controversies and resentment from affected nations.

Examples:

Spanish-American War (1898): The U.S. intervention in Cuba and the Philippines marked its emergence as a global power. However, the annexation of the Philippines and American influence in Cuba led to anti-American sentiments.

Vietnam War (1955-1975): The U.S. involvement in Vietnam during the Cold War sparked protests domestically and criticism internationally. The war left a deep impact on the perception of the U.S. as a global force.

Iraq War (2003): The invasion of Iraq, justified on grounds of weapons of mass destruction, faced widespread international criticism and strained relations with countries skeptical of the U.S. rationale.

Geopolitical Maneuvers: The Cold War and Beyond

The geopolitical landscape of the 20th century was dominated by the Cold War, a struggle for ideological supremacy between the United States and the Soviet Union. The U.S. engaged in geopolitical maneuvers to contain the spread of communism, leading to alliances, covert operations, and interventions. This section will scrutinize how these geopolitical maneuvers, while serving the interests of the U.S., may have contributed to negative perceptions among nations caught in the crossfire of superpower rivalry.

The Cold War era saw the United States engaged in geopolitical maneuvers to contain the spread of communism. Alliances, covert operations, and interventions defined this period, influencing global perceptions of the U.S. as it navigated the complexities of superpower rivalry.

Examples:

Marshall Plan (1948): The U.S. initiated the Marshall Plan to provide economic assistance to Western European countries, aiming to prevent the spread of communism. While it was successful, it also led to tensions with the Soviet Union.

Cuban Missile Crisis (1962): The intense standoff between the U.S. and the Soviet Union over missile deployments in Cuba heightened global tensions and showcased the geopolitical maneuvering of both superpowers.

Afghanistan (1980s): U.S. support for Afghan rebels against Soviet forces during the Cold War had long-term consequences, contributing to geopolitical instability in the region.

Legacy and Reverberations: Connecting the Dots

The historical events explored in this chapter have left a lasting legacy, shaping the narrative of the United States and influencing the perceptions of the global community. By connecting the dots between colonial history, wars, interventions, and geopolitical maneuvers, we aim to provide a nuanced understanding of the historical context that underlies contemporary criticisms. This exploration sets the stage for the subsequent chapters, offering a foundation for comprehending the complexities of the United States' standing in the world and the factors that contribute to dissent.

Politics, as a lens through which nations perceive one another, often shapes the ebb and flow of international relations. The United States, as a global superpower, has been both an architect and a subject of political discourse on the world stage. In this chapter, we delve into the intricate web of political motivations behind anti-American sentiment, exploring specific instances where political decisions and actions have fueled criticism from various quarters.

The Dynamics of Political Dissent

Political criticism towards the United States is a complex interplay of historical grievances, ideological clashes, and strategic considerations. Some nations harbor reservations about the perceived unilateralism and hegemony in U.S. foreign policy, while others critique specific decisions that impact global stability. Examining these political dynamics provides a nuanced understanding of why certain countries express dissent.

Examples:

Iran: The strained relationship between the U.S. and Iran dates back to the 1953 coup, where the U.S. played a role in overthrowing Iran's democratically elected Prime Minister Mohammad Mossadegh. The subsequent support for the Shah and the Iranian Revolution in 1979 fueled anti-American sentiments.

Venezuela: Political leaders in Venezuela, particularly during Hugo Chávez's presidency, criticized U.S. interventionism in Latin America. The perceived interference in regional affairs and opposition to leftist governments contributed to anti-American rhetoric.

North Korea: The Korean War (1950-1953) and the subsequent division of the Korean Peninsula left a lasting impact on U.S.-North Korea relations. Ongoing geopolitical tensions, combined with the U.S. military presence in the region, contribute to North Korea's anti-American stance.

Unilateralism and Hegemony: A Cause for Concern

One recurring theme in political criticism is the perception of U.S. unilateralism and hegemony in international affairs. Critics argue that the United States often acts without due consideration for the opinions and interests of other nations, leading to a sense of discontent among those who feel marginalized or disregarded.

Examples:

Iraq War (2003): The decision to invade Iraq, justified on the grounds of weapons of mass destruction, faced significant international opposition. Countries like France and Germany were vocal critics, asserting that the U.S. acted unilaterally without sufficient evidence.

International Criminal Court (ICC): The U.S.'s refusal to ratify the Rome Statute establishing the ICC and its objections to the court's jurisdiction over U.S. citizens reflect concerns about perceived infringements on national sovereignty.

Ideological Clashes: Democracy Promotion and Beyond

The promotion of democracy and human rights has been a cornerstone of U.S. foreign policy. However, this approach has led to ideological clashes with nations that may view it as a form of interference in their internal affairs. The tension between promoting democratic values and respecting the sovereignty of other nations underscores the complexity of political criticisms.

Examples:

Russia: The U.S. support for pro-democracy movements in Eastern Europe, including Ukraine, has been a source of tension with Russia. The perception of U.S. interference in the region contributes to strained relations.

China: U.S. criticisms of China's human rights record, particularly in Tibet and Xinjiang, have led to diplomatic tensions. China views such criticisms as interference in its domestic affairs.

Geostrategic Considerations: Balancing Alliances and Rivalries

Nations often navigate a delicate balance between alliances and rivalries in pursuit of their strategic interests. The United States, as a key player in global geopolitics, has at times aligned with certain nations while conflicting with others. These geopolitical considerations play a pivotal role in shaping political criticisms.

Examples:

Saudi Arabia: While the U.S. has maintained a strategic alliance with Saudi Arabia for decades, criticisms arise concerning human rights abuses, particularly in the context of the Saudi-led intervention in Yemen and the murder of journalist Jamal Khashoggi.

Cuba: The U.S. embargo on Cuba, initiated during the Cold War, has been a source of contention. Despite the changing global political landscape, the embargo persists, contributing to strained relations.

Economic Policies and Criticisms

Economic policies pursued by the United States also play a significant role in shaping political criticisms. Trade practices, sanctions, and economic dominance contribute to a complex web of international relations.

Examples:

European Union: Disagreements over trade policies, including tariffs imposed by the U.S. on European goods, have led to tensions with the European Union. The perceived unilateralism in trade decisions fuels political criticisms.

Latin American Nations: Criticisms of U.S. economic policies in Latin America, including neoliberal reforms and trade agreements, have fueled anti-American sentiments in the region.

Historical Resentments and Lingering Grievances

In addition to contemporary political decisions, historical resentments and lingering grievances contribute to political criticisms. Past actions, such as interventions and support for certain regimes, cast a long shadow over international perceptions of the United States.

Examples:

Guatemala: The U.S. involvement in the 1954 coup in Guatemala, which led to the overthrow of the democratically elected government, continues to influence political criticisms from Guatemala.

Philippines: The historical context of U.S. colonial rule in the Philippines, including events like the Philippine-American War, shapes contemporary criticisms and concerns about neocolonialism.

Navigating the Political Landscape

Political criticisms of the United States are embedded in a complex matrix of historical events, ideological clashes, and geopolitical considerations. As nations navigate the intricate terrain of global politics, the U.S. finds itself both a champion and a target of political discourse. Understanding the motivations behind political criticisms is essential for fostering diplomatic dialogue and addressing the root causes of dissent. In the subsequent sections, we will further examine disagreements on international policies and alliances, continuing the exploration of the multifaceted relationship between the United States and its global critics.

Examination of Disagreements on International Policies and Alliances

The global political landscape is a tapestry woven with diverse interests, conflicting ideologies, and strategic alliances. Disagreements on international policies and alliances often serve as flashpoints in diplomatic relations, shaping the perceptions nations hold of each other. In this section, we scrutinize instances where the United States' policy decisions and its alliances have been sources of contention, contributing to political criticisms from various countries and leaders.

Climate Change Policies: A Rift in Global Cooperation

Climate change, a critical global challenge, has been a significant point of contention between the United States and other nations. Disagreements on climate policies have fueled criticism, particularly regarding the U.S. withdrawal from the Paris Agreement during the administration of President Donald Trump.

Examples:

European Union: European leaders, including German Chancellor Angela Merkel and French President Emmanuel Macron, expressed disappointment and criticism when the U.S. announced its withdrawal from the Paris Agreement in 2017. The move strained transatlantic relations, with European nations emphasizing the importance of collective efforts to address climate change.

China: China, a key player in international climate efforts, has expressed concerns about the U.S. stance on climate change. Disagreements on environmental policies have underscored differences in priorities and approaches to addressing the global climate crisis.

Iran Nuclear Deal: Discord and Diplomatic Tensions

The Iran Nuclear Deal, officially known as the Joint Comprehensive Plan of Action (JCPOA), became a focal point of international diplomacy. The U.S.'s withdrawal from the agreement under the Trump administration and subsequent disagreements over its revival have strained relations with other signatory nations.

Examples:

European Signatories: European nations, including Germany, France, and the United Kingdom, expressed regret and concern when the U.S. withdrew from the JCPOA in 2018. Efforts to salvage the agreement without U.S. participation have highlighted diplomatic tensions and differences in approach to Iran.

Iran: The U.S. withdrawal and reimposition of sanctions prompted strong criticism from Iran. Disagreements over the JCPOA have contributed to heightened tensions in the region, showcasing the impact of divergent international policies on geopolitical stability.

Trade Policies and Tariffs: Economic Disputes and Global Strain

Trade policies, tariffs, and economic disputes have been significant contributors to political criticisms of the United States. The imposition of tariffs on imports, particularly in the context of trade wars, has sparked disagreements and strained relations with key trading partners.

Examples:

China: The U.S.-China trade war, initiated with the imposition of tariffs on goods, created a rift in economic relations. Chinese leaders, including President Xi Jinping, criticized the U.S. approach, leading to a protracted trade dispute with far-reaching implications for the global economy.

European Union: The imposition of tariffs on European goods by the U.S. prompted criticism from EU leaders, including European Commission President Ursula von der Leyen. Trade disputes and disagreements over economic policies have underscored the challenges of maintaining stable international economic relations.

NATO and Burden-Sharing: Strains in Transatlantic Relations

The North Atlantic Treaty Organization (NATO), a cornerstone of transatlantic security, has been a source of disagreements, particularly regarding burden-sharing and defense spending. Calls for NATO members to contribute more to collective defense have led to diplomatic tensions.

Examples:

European NATO Members: U.S. leaders, including President Donald Trump, criticized NATO members for perceived inadequacies in defense spending. European leaders, such as German Chancellor Angela Merkel, defended their contributions but acknowledged the need for increased defense expenditures. These disagreements have highlighted divergent views on the role and responsibilities of NATO members.

Turkey: Turkey's role within NATO has been a point of contention, particularly regarding its purchase of Russian S-400 missile defense systems. The U.S. response, including sanctions, underscores the challenges of balancing alliances with divergent security priorities.

Israel-Palestine Conflict: Diplomatic Shifts and Regional Dynamics

The Israel-Palestine conflict has been a longstanding and sensitive geopolitical issue. U.S. policies, including the recognition of Jerusalem as Israel's capital, have sparked criticism and strained relations with nations in the Middle East.

Examples:

Palestinian Leadership: The U.S. recognition of Jerusalem as Israel's capital faced strong condemnation from Palestinian leaders, including President Mahmoud Abbas. Disagreements over the approach to the Israel-Palestine conflict have complicated diplomatic efforts in the region.

Arab Nations: Some Arab nations, while maintaining diplomatic ties with the U.S., have expressed concerns about the impact of U.S. policies on regional stability. Disagreements over the Israel-Palestine conflict highlight the intricacies of managing alliances in the Middle East.

Migration Policies: Humanitarian Concerns and Global Critique

U.S. policies on immigration and asylum-seeking have generated international criticism, particularly regarding issues of human rights and humanitarian concerns. Disagreements on migration policies have strained relations with nations and organizations advocating for more inclusive approaches.

Examples:

United Nations: The U.S. withdrawal from the United Nations Human Rights Council (UNHRC) in 2018 was met with criticism from international leaders. Disagreements over the treatment of migrants and refugees highlighted the challenges of aligning U.S. policies with global human rights standards.

Latin American Nations: U.S. immigration policies, including family separations, faced strong criticism from Latin American nations. Disagreements over the treatment of migrants at the U.S.-Mexico border have strained regional relations and fueled calls for a more humanitarian approach.

Cybersecurity and Digital Governance: Emerging Frontiers of Dispute

As the world becomes increasingly connected, issues related to cybersecurity and digital governance have emerged as new frontiers of disagreement. Differences in approaches to digital policies and cyber threats have fueled tensions in the realm of international relations.

Examples:

China: The U.S.-China rivalry extends into the digital realm, with disagreements over cybersecurity, intellectual property theft, and technology competition. The U.S. has criticized China's digital practices, leading to ongoing tensions in economic and technological spheres.

European Union: Differences in digital governance approaches between the U.S. and the European Union, including issues of data privacy and antitrust concerns, have led to disagreements. The EU's efforts to establish independent digital regulations highlight the complexities of aligning policies in the digital age.

Global Health Governance: Responses to Pandemics and Vaccine Diplomacy

The COVID-19 pandemic has brought global health governance to the forefront, with differing responses and approaches to vaccine distribution. Disagreements over pandemic management and vaccine diplomacy have influenced international perceptions.

Examples:

World Health Organization (WHO): The U.S. decision to withdraw from the WHO under the Trump administration and subsequent reengagement under President Joe Biden underscored disagreements over the organization's role in global health governance.

Global Vaccine Distribution: Disparities in global vaccine distribution and debates over intellectual property rights have led to disagreements between the U.S. and other nations. Calls for more equitable access to vaccines highlight the challenges of coordinating international responses to health crises.

Navigating the Diplomatic Maze

Disagreements on international policies and alliances constitute a complex terrain where nations negotiate divergent interests, ideologies, and strategic priorities. The United States, as a global actor, finds itself at the center of these diplomatic intricacies, where each decision carries implications for its standing in the world. Understanding the multifaceted nature of these disagreements provides a lens through which to comprehend the intricacies of political criticisms directed at the United States. As we continue our exploration, the subsequent chapters will delve into economic factors, cultural clashes, and military interventions, unraveling the layers of dissent that contribute to the complex tapestry of global relations.

Chapter 3: Economic Factors: Navigating Disparities and Global Impact

In the grand tapestry of global relations, the economic threads woven by the United States create a complex and often controversial narrative. On the surface, the U.S. stands as an economic juggernaut, shaping the contours of international commerce and finance. However, beneath this veneer of prosperity lies a tale of disparities that span both domestic landscapes and the interconnected world stage.

Economic Disparities: A Tale of Two Realities

Within the United States, the glittering façade of economic prosperity coexists with the shadows of stark disparities. These disparities manifest along various fault lines, creating a narrative that sparks both domestic debates and international critiques.

In the American heartland, urban centers pulse with innovation, technological advancements, and economic prosperity. The skylines of cities like New York and San Francisco testify to a narrative of growth and affluence. However, beyond the urban glow, pockets of the nation grapple with economic challenges, painting a picture of inequality.

The income gap, a chasm that has widened over the years, raises eyebrows both within and beyond America's borders. Figures like Senator Bernie Sanders and movements like Occupy Wall Street have brought attention to the unequal distribution of wealth, framing it not just as an economic concern but as a matter of social justice.

Yet, the disparities extend beyond income brackets. Racial and ethnic lines intersect with economic struggles, creating an uneven playing field where systemic biases perpetuate inequality. The Black Lives Matter movement, initially focused on racial injustice in policing, has expanded its lens to critique the systemic economic inequalities that disproportionately affect Black communities.

The regional divides further deepen the narrative. While urban hubs thrive, rural areas face economic challenges, highlighting the uneven distribution of resources and opportunities. The Rust Belt, once the heartbeat of traditional industries, now bears the scars of economic decline, standing in contrast to the growth seen in the Sun Belt.

Internationally, these disparities become a focal point of criticism. Critics argue that the U.S., despite its economic prowess, has not fully addressed domestic inequalities, challenging the notion of the American Dream and equal opportunity.

Global Economic Impact: The Ripple Effect of U.S. Power

As the world's economic giant, the United States casts a far-reaching shadow that extends beyond its borders. Its economic policies, trade practices, and financial institutions shape the interconnected web of international commerce, finance, and development.

The U.S. dollar reigns supreme on the global stage, holding the coveted position of the world's primary reserve currency. This dollar dominance facilitates global trade and financial transactions, creating both opportunities and challenges. However, critics argue that this economic clout can be wielded as a tool for coercion, as seen in the imposition of sanctions and trade policies.

The technological landscape, dominated by Silicon Valley and tech behemoths, is another arena where the U.S. holds sway. Innovations from American tech companies shape the digital world and influence economies worldwide. While this technological hegemony fosters progress, it also raises concerns about privacy, data security, and the concentration of power.

Trade imbalances, a byproduct of the U.S.'s major role in international trade, have become points of contention. The U.S.-China trade relationship, marked by imbalances, intellectual property concerns, and market access issues, takes center stage in global economic discussions. The U.S. participation in trade agreements, such as NAFTA and the USMCA, further shapes regional economic dynamics.

The U.S. is also a significant player in global aid and development assistance. Its contributions to international aid programs, focused on health, education, and infrastructure, aim to foster global development. However, critics argue that the conditions attached to aid can perpetuate dependency and influence the policies of recipient nations.

Within international financial institutions like the IMF and World Bank, the U.S. wields influence, shaping global economic policies. However, concerns about debt diplomacy and conditional lending draw scrutiny, reflecting power dynamics in the realm of global finance.

Navigating Economic Waters

Economic factors form a labyrinthine network that intertwines the fate of nations and shapes the narratives that define them. The United States, with its economic prowess and internal disparities, occupies a central role in this complex dance. The disparities within the nation and its economic impact on the global stage create a dynamic landscape that elicits both admiration and criticism.

As we move forward, delving into the critique of economic policies and trade practices, we will continue to unravel the layers of dissent that contribute to the intricate relationship between the United States and its global critics. The economic story of the U.S. is one of influence, power, and, at times, contentious disparities that reverberate across borders, shaping the way nations perceive and interact with this economic powerhouse.

Critique of Economic Policies and Trade Practices: Navigating the Controversies

As we journey through the intricate world of global relations, the economic policies and trade practices of the United States emerge as a focal point of contention. While the U.S. stands as an economic juggernaut, its strategies in economic governance and global trade are not without critics. In this chapter, we unravel the complexities, exploring the critiques that echo both domestically and on the international stage.

1. Trade Practices: Balancing Act or Economic Coercion?

Trade, the lifeblood of the global economy, is a terrain where the U.S. wields significant influence. Yet, the methods employed in this economic arena draw both admiration and skepticism.

At the forefront of global trade discussions is the U.S.-China relationship. The trade war that unfolded between these economic giants was marked by tariff impositions, creating ripples across industries and economies. Critics argue that such confrontations can disrupt global supply chains, stifle economic growth, and contribute to an atmosphere of uncertainty.

The negotiation and renegotiation of trade agreements, such as NAFTA and the USMCA, invite scrutiny. While these pacts aim to foster regional economic cooperation, critics point to potential imbalances and question whether they truly address the needs of all participating nations. The impacts on industries, workers, and environmental standards become focal points of contention.

Beyond specific trade agreements, the broader question of fair trade practices surfaces. Accusations of currency manipulation, intellectual property theft, and market access disparities have been leveled against trading partners, adding layers of complexity to global economic relationships. Critics argue that addressing these issues is crucial for creating a level playing field that benefits all participants.

2. Economic Policies: Inequality, Innovation, and Intervention

The economic policies of the United States, crafted to steer the nation's prosperity, are subject to a nuanced critique that spans issues of inequality, innovation, and governmental intervention.

Income inequality, a persistent challenge domestically, draws sharp criticism. The tax policies implemented over the years come under scrutiny, with debates centering on whether they perpetuate or alleviate economic disparities. Calls for progressive taxation and comprehensive welfare programs underscore a push for economic policies that prioritize equity.

Innovation, a hallmark of the U.S. economy, also draws its share of critiques. The dominance of tech giants raises concerns about monopolistic practices, data privacy, and the concentration of economic power. While technological advancements fuel progress, critics argue for regulatory frameworks that prevent abuses and ensure a fair competitive landscape.

Governmental intervention, particularly in times of economic crises, raises questions about the balance between free-market principles and the need for regulatory oversight. The response to the 2008 financial crisis, marked by bailouts and stimulus packages, invites analysis of the long-term implications on economic stability and the role of government in shaping economic outcomes.

3. Global Aid and Development Assistance: Altruism or Influence?

The U.S. role in global aid and development assistance is a subject of both commendation and suspicion. While the contributions made to international programs aim to foster global development, the motivations behind such assistance come under the microscope.

Critics question the conditional nature of U.S. aid, highlighting instances where economic and political considerations influence the distribution of assistance. The notion of "debt diplomacy" arises, suggesting that aid can be leveraged to advance U.S. interests, creating dependencies and shaping the policies of recipient nations.

Within international financial institutions like the IMF and World Bank, where the U.S. holds considerable influence, concerns are voiced about power dynamics. Critics argue that the decision-making processes may disproportionately favor the interests of major economies, potentially perpetuating global economic inequalities.

4. Environmental Impact and Sustainability: A Growing Imperative

As the world grapples with the challenges of climate change, the environmental impact of economic policies becomes a critical consideration. The U.S., as a major global player, faces critiques related to its approach to sustainability and environmental responsibility.

Withdrawals from international agreements, such as the Paris Agreement, draw criticism for signaling a lack of commitment to global environmental initiatives. Critics argue that such actions hinder collective efforts to address climate change and tarnish the nation's reputation as a leader in sustainable practices.

Domestically, debates surrounding energy policies, regulation of emissions, and support for renewable energy sources underscore the tension between economic interests and environmental stewardship. Advocates for more aggressive climate action call for policies that prioritize sustainability and contribute to the global fight against environmental degradation.

5. Social and Cultural Impact: Beyond Economic Numbers

Critiques of economic policies and trade practices extend beyond fiscal measures, delving into their societal and cultural impacts. The commodification of culture, labor practices, and the role of corporations in shaping social narratives emerge as areas of concern.

The influence of multinational corporations in shaping cultural norms and values is met with skepticism. Critics argue that the pursuit of profit can sometimes come at the expense of ethical considerations, leading to practices that exploit labor, perpetuate cultural stereotypes, and prioritize financial gain over social responsibility.

Labor practices within and outside U.S. borders also face scrutiny. From concerns about outsourcing to debates over fair wages and workers' rights, the economic policies that govern the workplace become intertwined with social justice considerations.

6. Global Leadership and Soft Power: A Double-Edged Sword

The U.S., as a global economic powerhouse, wields soft power through its economic influence. However, this influence can be a double-edged sword, eliciting both admiration and critiques.

The role of the U.S. in shaping international norms and standards is applauded when aligned with principles of democracy, human rights, and global cooperation. However, deviations from these ideals, such as support for authoritarian regimes or actions perceived as undermining international cooperation, draw criticism and challenge the nation's position as a global leader.

The critique of U.S. economic policies and trade practices navigates a complex landscape shaped by competing interests, ethical considerations, and the ever-evolving dynamics of the global economy. As we continue our exploration, the subsequent chapters will delve into cultural clashes, military interventions, and the broader implications of dissent, unraveling the layers that contribute to the intricate relationship between the United States and its global critics.

Chapter 4: Cultural and Ideological Differences: Navigating the Global Mosaic

In the vast tapestry of global relations, cultural and ideological differences emerge as threads that weave through the intricate relationship between the United States and its global counterparts. As we embark on this exploration, we'll navigate the nuances of cultural clashes, understanding the diverse values that shape perceptions and contribute to the complex interplay of nations.

1. Cultural Clashes: Where Worlds Collide

Cultural clashes are not merely points of friction; they are the intersection where diverse worldviews, traditions, and norms collide. The United States, with its rich tapestry of cultures, encounters challenges when its values encounter those rooted in different histories and belief systems.

One poignant example is the clash of individualism versus collectivism. The American ethos often celebrates individual freedom, self-expression, and personal success. However, in cultures where community, family, and collective well-being take precedence, this emphasis on individualism can be perceived as a departure from shared values.

Cultural clashes also extend to attitudes towards authority, hierarchy, and social structures. The egalitarian ideals championed in the U.S. may clash with societies where hierarchical structures are deeply ingrained. These clashes can manifest in diplomatic tensions, debates over governance models, and differing expectations in international partnerships.

Religious diversity, a hallmark of the U.S., can also be a source of tension. The secular nature of American society contrasts with regions where religious identity plays a central role in shaping cultural norms. This contrast can lead to misunderstandings, with the U.S. being perceived as either overly secular or insensitive to religious considerations.

The celebration of diversity within the U.S. can also be a source of tension when exported abroad. The American model of multiculturalism may be met with skepticism or resistance in regions where cultural homogeneity is viewed as a source of social cohesion.

2. Values in Flux: Navigating Evolving Norms

As cultural landscapes evolve, so do the values that underpin societies. The clash of traditional values and evolving norms poses a challenge in international relations, where perceptions of the United States are often shaped by the pace and nature of societal change.

Issues related to gender equality, LGBTQ+ rights, and changing family structures exemplify areas where evolving American norms may differ from entrenched cultural expectations. While strides towards inclusivity are celebrated domestically, these shifts can generate resistance in societies where traditional gender roles and family structures are deeply ingrained.

The promotion of human rights, a core tenet of American values, can also be a source of contention. While the U.S. advocates for universal principles of democracy and human dignity, differing cultural perspectives on governance and individual freedoms may lead to disagreements over the application of these values in international contexts.

Environmental consciousness, another evolving value within the U.S., can be a point of conflict when engaging with nations where economic development is prioritized over environmental sustainability. Disagreements over approaches to climate change and resource management highlight the clash of values in the pursuit of global cooperation.

3. Soft Power and American Influence: The Cultural Export

The influence of American pop culture and media is a formidable force that shapes perceptions, fuels trends, and permeates societies across the globe. This cultural export, often referred to as "soft power," is a significant aspect of the U.S.'s global presence.

From Hollywood blockbusters to chart-topping music, American pop culture is a global phenomenon. The ubiquity of American films, television shows, and music creates a shared cultural language that transcends borders. However, the impact of this cultural export is not uniform, and reactions vary across different societies.

In some regions, the influence of American pop culture is embraced, reflecting a shared enthusiasm for the creativity and innovation emanating from the entertainment industry. In other contexts, there may be resistance, with concerns about cultural imperialism, the erosion of local traditions, and the influence of Western values.

The proliferation of social media platforms amplifies the reach of American pop culture, shaping the aspirations and lifestyles of individuals worldwide. Fashion trends, consumer preferences, and even linguistic expressions often bear the imprint of American cultural influence.

However, the impact of American soft power is not without complexities. Cultural appropriation, stereotypes perpetuated by media representations, and the commodification of cultural symbols are critiques that arise in the wake of this cultural export. The influence of American media, while a powerful force, is a double-edged sword that invites both admiration and skepticism.

Bridging the Cultural Gulf

As we navigate the terrain of cultural and ideological differences, it becomes evident that the global stage is not a monolithic space but a mosaic of diverse perspectives, values, and histories. The United States, as a cultural powerhouse, contributes both to the richness of this mosaic and the challenges of navigating its complexities.

Cultural clashes and differences in values offer opportunities for dialogue, understanding, and mutual enrichment. By acknowledging the diversity of cultural landscapes and respecting the agency of nations to shape their destinies, diplomatic efforts can move beyond friction towards collaboration.

As we move forward in our exploration, the subsequent chapters will delve into the impact of military interventions, economic strategies, and the broader implications of dissent. Through this journey, we aim to unravel the layers that contribute to the intricate relationship between the United States and its global critics, recognizing that understanding and bridging cultural gulfs is an essential step towards fostering meaningful international relations.

The Global Impact of American Pop Culture and Media:
Shaping Minds, Bridging Divides

In the interconnected world of the 21st century, American pop culture and media have become influential forces that transcend geographical boundaries, shaping the way people think, communicate, and perceive the world. As we delve into the impact of this cultural export, we'll explore how American movies, music, television shows, and digital content influence societies, fuel global trends, and contribute to the intricate dynamics of international relations.

1. Hollywood and Beyond: The Cinematic Influence

Hollywood, often referred to as the entertainment capital of the world, serves as a powerful engine of cultural influence. American films, known for their high production values, captivating storytelling, and cutting-edge technology, reach audiences far and wide.

The global success of Hollywood blockbusters contributes not only to the economic prosperity of the American film industry but also to the dissemination of American values, lifestyle, and perspectives. From superhero epics to heartwarming dramas, these films create a shared cultural experience that transcends language barriers.

American filmmakers tackle universal themes that resonate with audiences globally, fostering a sense of commonality. However, this cinematic influence is not without its challenges. Critics argue that the dominance of Hollywood can lead to cultural homogenization, overshadowing local film industries and perpetuating certain stereotypes.

2. The Soundtrack of Global Culture: American Music Worldwide

American music, with its diversity and innovation, has become a global soundtrack that permeates the airwaves from Tokyo to Buenos Aires. Genres like pop, hip-hop, rock, and jazz have crossed borders, creating a shared musical vocabulary that unites people of different cultures.

The influence of American music is not limited to its sound but extends to its impact on fashion, language, and societal norms. Artists like Beyoncé, Taylor Swift, and Kendrick Lamar, among others, have not only topped charts but have also shaped conversations about identity, social justice, and personal empowerment.

While American music is celebrated for its creativity and global appeal, there are critiques. Some argue that the dominance of Western music can marginalize local musical traditions. Others highlight concerns about cultural appropriation and the commercialization of diverse musical styles.

3. Television Shows: Breaking Down Cultural Barriers

American television shows, ranging from sitcoms to dramas and reality TV, have become cultural ambassadors that introduce audiences to American life, humor, and societal dynamics. Shows like "Friends," "Breaking Bad," and "The Simpsons" have gained international acclaim, transcending cultural differences.

The availability of American TV shows on streaming platforms has further accelerated their global reach. Audiences around the world binge-watch series that provide glimpses into American culture, relationships, and societal issues. This accessibility fosters a sense of familiarity and connection.

However, the representation of American life in TV shows can be a double-edged sword. While it introduces audiences to diverse perspectives, there are concerns about the portrayal of stereotypes and the selective narrative focus that may not capture the complexities of American society.

4. Digital Age Dominance: Social Media and Beyond

In the digital age, the influence of American pop culture has found new frontiers in the realm of social media and online content. Platforms like Facebook, Twitter, Instagram, and YouTube amplify the reach of American trends, memes, and influencers, creating a global digital conversation.

The rise of American influencers and content creators contributes to the projection of American lifestyles and values. Beauty standards, fashion trends, and lifestyle choices showcased on digital platforms become aspirational for audiences worldwide. The immediacy of social media connects people across continents in real-time, fostering a sense of global community.

However, the digital age also brings forth challenges. The spread of misinformation, the potential for cultural insensitivity, and the dominance of certain narratives can create tensions. Social media platforms, while connecting the world, also become arenas for ideological clashes and debates.

5. The Soft Power Paradox: Admiration and Skepticism

The influence of American pop culture and media, often described as "soft power," is a significant aspect of the nation's global presence. Soft power, rooted in attraction rather than coercion, has the potential to shape perceptions, foster goodwill, and build cultural bridges.

The global embrace of American pop culture is evident in the popularity of American brands, fashion trends, and entertainment franchises. However, this soft power is not universally embraced. Skepticism exists, with concerns about cultural imperialism, the erosion of local traditions, and the potential for American values to overshadow indigenous cultures.

Navigating the soft power paradox requires an understanding of the delicate balance between cultural influence and respect for diversity. While American pop culture has the capacity to bring people together through shared experiences, it also requires a nuanced approach that acknowledges the complexity of global cultural dynamics.

A Cultural Tapestry in Flux

As we conclude our exploration of the influence of American pop culture and media, we recognize that the global impact is both a reflection of cultural dynamism and a catalyst for evolving societal norms. American creativity, innovation, and storytelling prowess have forged connections and ignited imaginations around the world.

The influence of American pop culture and media is not a unidirectional force but a dynamic interplay of reception, reinterpretation, and response. It is a testament to the interconnectedness of the modern world, where cultural boundaries are porous, and the exchange of ideas is a constant dialogue.

As we journey forward, the subsequent chapters will delve into the impact of military interventions, economic strategies, and the broader implications of dissent. Through this exploration, we aim to unravel the layers that contribute to the intricate relationship between the United States and its global critics, recognizing that cultural influence is a powerful force that shapes the narratives of nations.

Chapter 5: Military Interventions: Unraveling the Threads of Global Impact

In the annals of history, the United States has been a protagonist in various military interventions abroad, shaping the course of nations and the dynamics of global relations. In this chapter, we embark on an exploration of U.S. military actions, seeking to understand the complexities, motivations, and the ripple effects that extend far beyond borders.

1. The Arsenal of Democracy: A Brief Historical Prelude

To comprehend the roots of U.S. military interventions, we must glance at history's pages. From the beaches of Normandy during World War II to the jungles of Vietnam, the United States has, at times, assumed the role of a global peacekeeper, a defender of democracy, and a counterforce against perceived threats.

The Cold War era marked a significant chapter, with the U.S. engaging in proxy conflicts to contain the spread of communism. The Korean War and the Vietnam War, both influenced by the ideological struggle between superpowers, left indelible marks on the landscape of military interventions.

The end of the Cold War did not signal a retreat from global affairs for the U.S. Instead, it ushered in an era of interventions driven by diverse factors, including regional conflicts, humanitarian crises, and the pursuit of national security interests.

2. The Gulf Wars: Shaping the Middle East Landscape

The Gulf Wars, particularly the First Gulf War in 1990-1991 and the Second Gulf War in 2003, marked pivotal moments in U.S. military interventions. The liberation of Kuwait and the ousting of Saddam Hussein were catalysts that reshaped the geopolitical dynamics of the Middle East.

While the First Gulf War enjoyed broad international support, the Second Gulf War sparked debates about the legitimacy of intervention and the long-term consequences of regime change. These interventions ignited sectarian tensions, reshaped alliances, and set the stage for subsequent conflicts in the region.

3. The War on Terror: A Global Battlefield

The September 11, 2001 attacks thrust the United States into a new paradigm of military intervention: the War on Terror. Afghanistan became the primary theater, with the goal of dismantling the Taliban regime and eradicating the terrorist infrastructure.

The invasion of Iraq in 2003, justified by intelligence suggesting weapons of mass destruction, became a defining moment. The prolonged conflict that ensued had profound consequences, from the loss of lives to the destabilization of the region. The narrative surrounding the justification for intervention became a source of international scrutiny and domestic debate.

Military interventions also extended to other theaters, with drone strikes and special operations becoming tools in the fight against terrorist networks. The War on Terror, with its global reach, raised questions about the balance between security imperatives and respect for sovereignty.

4. Humanitarian Interventions: The Thin Line Between Aid and Intervention

Humanitarian crises, marked by atrocities and widespread suffering, have compelled the U.S. to intervene on grounds of moral imperative. The interventions in Bosnia and Kosovo during the Balkans conflict in the 1990s aimed to prevent ethnic cleansing and restore stability.

The intervention in Libya in 2011, framed as a response to impending atrocities, raised debates about the scope and consequences of military interventions based on humanitarian grounds. The aftermath of such interventions, including questions about nation-building and the responsibility to protect, underscores the complex nature of humanitarian interventions.

5. Dilemmas and Debates: The Costs of Military Interventions

Military interventions, regardless of motivations, come with profound costs. Human lives lost, economic resources expended, and the long-term repercussions on the affected regions are dimensions that demand scrutiny.

The toll on military personnel, both physically and psychologically, raises questions about the ethical dimensions of interventions. The deployment of troops in far-flung regions and the extended duration of conflicts challenge notions of just war and the duty to protect.

Economic considerations also loom large. The financial burdens of sustained military interventions can strain national budgets, leading to debates about priorities and the allocation of resources. The opportunity costs, both in terms of domestic investments and global diplomacy, become part of the calculus.

6. The Unintended Consequences: Navigating the Aftermath

One of the defining features of military interventions is the unpredictable nature of their aftermath. While interventions may achieve immediate objectives, the long-term consequences can be far-reaching and, at times, unexpected.

Nation-building efforts, aimed at establishing stable governance structures, have encountered challenges. The delicate balance between fostering local agency and imposing external models raises questions about the sustainability of interventions. The experiences of Iraq and Afghanistan underscore the complexities of post-conflict reconstruction.

The destabilizing impact of interventions on regional dynamics is another facet. Sectarian tensions, power vacuums, and the rise of non-state actors can reshape the geopolitical landscape, with repercussions extending beyond the immediate theater of conflict.

Navigating the Complex Terrain

Military interventions, etched into the history of the United States, are a complex and multifaceted aspect of its global role. As we navigate the terrain of U.S. military actions abroad, we encounter dilemmas, debates, and the enduring quest for a balance between national interests and global stability.

In the subsequent chapters, we will delve into the impact of military interventions on global stability and sovereignty concerns. The exploration will unveil the intricate layers that contribute to the complex relationship between the United States and its global critics. Understanding the motivations, consequences, and ethical dimensions of military interventions is essential for grappling with the challenges of a world where geopolitical dynamics are in constant flux.

Impact on Global Stability and Sovereignty Concerns: Balancing Act in a Shifting Landscape

As we delve deeper into the repercussions of U.S. military interventions, it becomes imperative to examine their impact on global stability and the concerns raised regarding national sovereignty. The intricacies of navigating this terrain are multifaceted, involving geopolitical shifts, ethical considerations, and the perpetual quest for a delicate equilibrium between national interests and international order.

1. Geopolitical Dynamics: Shaping the Chessboard

U.S. military interventions are seismic events that reverberate across the geopolitical chessboard, altering alliances, power structures, and regional dynamics. The repercussions of interventions, whether in the Middle East, the Balkans, or elsewhere, have far-reaching consequences that extend beyond the immediate theater of conflict.

Shifts in the balance of power, the rise of new regional players, and the realignment of alliances are common outcomes. The intervention in Iraq, for example, not only removed Saddam Hussein but also created a power vacuum that fueled sectarian tensions and contributed to the rise of non-state actors, fundamentally reshaping the dynamics of the Middle East.

While interventions may achieve short-term objectives, their long-term impact on global stability requires careful consideration. The unintended consequences of altered geopolitical landscapes underscore the need for strategic foresight in international relations.

2. Sovereignty Concerns: Navigating the Boundaries

The principle of national sovereignty, a cornerstone of international relations, becomes a focal point of debate and concern in the context of military interventions. The act of intervening in the affairs of another nation raises questions about the limits of sovereignty, the responsibility to protect, and the ethical dimensions of external interference.

The concept of the Responsibility to Protect (R2P) has been invoked to justify interventions on humanitarian grounds. While the intention is to prevent mass atrocities, the application of R2P involves navigating a delicate balance between the duty to protect vulnerable populations and the respect for the sovereignty of nations.

Critics argue that military interventions, even when framed as humanitarian endeavors, can be perceived as violations of sovereignty. The notion of external actors determining the fate of a nation raises concerns about the potential for neocolonialism and the imposition of foreign values on indigenous societies.

3. Regional Stability: Domino Effects and Power Vacuums

The impact of military interventions on regional stability is a multifaceted puzzle. While interventions may be driven by a desire to restore order or dismantle perceived threats, the aftermath can create power vacuums, fuel insurgency, and contribute to the spread of instability.

The intervention in Libya in 2011, for instance, aimed at preventing atrocities, led to the removal of Muammar Gaddafi. However, the power vacuum that ensued contributed to factionalism, the rise of armed groups, and the destabilization of the region. The ripple effects of such interventions can extend far beyond the borders of the nation in question.

Regional stability concerns also intersect with broader geopolitical considerations. The intervention in Syria, amid a complex web of alliances and proxy conflicts, illustrates how military actions can become entangled in regional power struggles, exacerbating tensions and complicating diplomatic solutions.

4. Ethical Considerations: The Human Cost and Moral Dilemmas

The ethical dimensions of military interventions cast a long shadow over the international stage. The human cost, in terms of lives lost, displaced populations, and the trauma endured by communities, is a haunting consequence that demands reflection.

The justifiability of military interventions, particularly in conflicts framed as preemptive or in pursuit of national security interests, raises moral dilemmas. The loss of civilian lives, the unintended consequences of intervention, and the challenges of post-conflict reconstruction become ethical quandaries that policymakers must grapple with.

Ethical considerations also extend to questions of transparency, accountability, and the adherence to international law. The use of force, whether authorized by international bodies or pursued unilaterally, is subject to scrutiny, with debates about the legality of interventions shaping perceptions and diplomatic relations.

5. Multilateralism vs. Unilateralism: Diplomatic Complexities

The approach to military interventions, whether undertaken unilaterally or through multilateral alliances, introduces another layer of complexity. Unilateral interventions, as seen in the invasion of Iraq in 2003, can strain diplomatic relations, erode trust, and create divisions within the international community.

Multilateral interventions, when conducted under the auspices of international organizations or coalitions, seek to garner broader support and legitimacy. However, the challenges of achieving consensus among diverse nations, each with its own interests and priorities, add a diplomatic dimension to the complexities of military interventions.

The tension between unilateralism and multilateralism becomes a reflection of broader debates about the role of international institutions, the distribution of power, and the effectiveness of collective action in addressing global challenges.

Navigating the Aftermath

As we conclude our exploration of the impact of U.S. military interventions on global stability and sovereignty concerns, the intricate layers of this complex terrain become apparent. The geopolitical shifts, ethical considerations, and diplomatic complexities underscore the multifaceted nature of military interventions and their enduring impact on the world stage.

Chapter 6: Perceptions of Arrogance: Unraveling the Complex Narrative

In the tapestry of global relations, perceptions play a pivotal role in shaping diplomatic interactions and influencing international attitudes. The United States, as a major global player, has been subject to various perceptions, and one recurring theme is the accusation of arrogance or hegemony. In this chapter, we embark on an analysis of how the U.S. is perceived in this light, exploring the complexities of the narrative that paints the nation as wielding undue influence and acting unilaterally on the world stage.

1. The Power Paradigm: A Double-Edged Sword

The United States, as a superpower, occupies a unique position in global affairs. Its economic, military, and cultural influence is unparalleled, marking it as a force capable of shaping international events. However, the very attributes that define its power become a source of contention, with some perceiving a sense of arrogance in how that power is wielded.

The concept of American exceptionalism, the belief in the nation's unique role and responsibility in global affairs, can contribute to perceptions of exceptional arrogance. While rooted in a sense of national pride, it can be interpreted as a form of exceptionalism that places the U.S. above international norms and obligations.

2. Unilateral Decision-Making: Navigating the Power Play

A significant source of perceptions of arrogance revolves around the issue of unilateral decision-making. Instances where the U.S. acts independently, without seeking broad international consensus, can be viewed through the lens of hegemony.

The invasion of Iraq in 2003 serves as a poignant example. The decision to use military force without explicit authorization from the United Nations Security Council sparked international condemnation. Critics argue that such unilateral actions disregard the principles of collective security and undermine the authority of international institutions.

While unilateral decisions may be driven by perceived national interests, they also amplify perceptions of the U.S. as an actor that operates outside the bounds of collective decision-making. The balance between national autonomy and international cooperation becomes a delicate diplomatic dance.

3. Disregard for International Opinions: Navigating the Diplomatic Landscape

The perception of arrogance is often intertwined with the notion of disregarding international opinions. Instances where the U.S. is perceived as unresponsive or dismissive of the perspectives of other nations contribute to a narrative of hegemony.

Trade policies, climate change agreements, and diplomatic negotiations are arenas where this perception comes to the forefront. The decision to withdraw from international agreements, such as the Paris Agreement on climate change, can be interpreted as prioritizing national interests over global cooperation.

Critics argue that a disregard for international opinions not only erodes trust but also reinforces perceptions of a power that acts unilaterally, imposing its will on the international community. The challenge lies in finding a balance between advancing national interests and respecting the diverse perspectives of a multipolar world.

4. The Challenge of Soft Power: Cultural Diplomacy Amid Critiques

Soft power, the ability to shape preferences through appeal and attraction, is a significant aspect of a nation's influence. However, even cultural diplomacy can become a source of perceived arrogance when not executed with nuance.

The global influence of American pop culture, technology, and educational institutions can be seen as both a positive force and a potential source of cultural imperialism. The ubiquity of American media, technology, and educational systems can contribute to the perception that the U.S. seeks to homogenize global cultures under its own influence.

The challenge lies in leveraging soft power to build bridges rather than fueling perceptions of cultural dominance. Acknowledging the diversity of global cultures and fostering genuine exchanges can mitigate the perception of cultural arrogance.

5. Balancing National Interests and Global Responsibilities: A Diplomatic Tightrope

Perceptions of arrogance often emerge from the delicate dance between national interests and global responsibilities. Striking the right balance requires navigating a diplomatic tightrope, recognizing the realities of power dynamics while upholding principles of international cooperation.

Multilateralism becomes a key instrument in this endeavor. Engaging with international institutions, seeking consensus on critical issues, and demonstrating a commitment to collaborative decision-making can counter perceptions of unilateralism and arrogance.

Diplomatic gestures that underscore a genuine commitment to global cooperation, such as participating in international forums and respecting international law, contribute to a narrative of responsible global leadership. Engaging in dialogue rather than imposing solutions reinforces a vision of the U.S. as a partner rather than a hegemonic force.

6. Shaping Perceptions through Policy Adjustments: A Call for Reflection

As the U.S. navigates the complex terrain of perceptions, there is an opportunity for policy adjustments that reflect a nuanced understanding of the global landscape. Reevaluating approaches to international agreements, emphasizing diplomacy over coercion, and acknowledging the importance of global perspectives can contribute to a recalibration of perceptions.

The challenge lies in recognizing that perceptions are dynamic and responsive to policy shifts. By fostering a narrative of humility, openness to diverse viewpoints, and a commitment to shared global goals, the U.S. can shape perceptions that align with its ideals of democracy, cooperation, and respect for international norms.

Conclusion: Navigating the Perception Paradox

In concluding our exploration of perceptions of arrogance, we recognize the intricacies of the narrative that paints the United States as a hegemonic force. Perceptions are shaped by a myriad of factors, including historical experiences, policy decisions, and cultural interactions. Navigating the perception paradox requires a nuanced understanding of power dynamics, a commitment to multilateralism, and a willingness to adapt diplomatic strategies to an ever-evolving global landscape.

Navigating the Diplomatic Maze: Critiquing Unilateral Decision-Making and the Perception of Disregard for International Opinions

In the intricate dance of global diplomacy, how a nation wields its power and engages with the international community shapes perceptions and influences the delicate fabric of relations. In this chapter, we delve into the critiques surrounding U.S. unilateral decision-making and the perceived disregard for international opinions, unpacking the complexities of these actions and their impact on the world stage.

1. The Solo Act: Unraveling Unilateral Decision-Making

Unilateral decision-making, where a nation acts independently without seeking broad international consensus, is a contentious issue that often raises eyebrows in the global arena. The accusation of going solo in decision-making can spark concerns about a nation acting without due regard for the perspectives and interests of others.

One example etched in recent history is the U.S. invasion of Iraq in 2003. The decision to use military force without explicit approval from the United Nations Security Council drew international criticism, with many arguing that such actions undermine the principles of collective security and the authority of international institutions.

Critics suggest that unilateral decisions can project an image of a nation acting with unchecked power, potentially eroding trust and cooperation on the global stage. The challenge lies in finding a balance between asserting national interests and fostering international collaboration.

2. The Diplomatic Tightrope: Disregarding International Opinions

Perceptions of disregard for international opinions often arise when a nation appears unresponsive or dismissive of the perspectives of others. This critique becomes particularly pronounced in areas such as trade policies, climate change agreements, and diplomatic negotiations.

The decision to withdraw from international agreements, like the Paris Agreement on climate change, can be seen as prioritizing national interests over global cooperation. Critics argue that such actions not only hinder progress on shared challenges but also contribute to a narrative of a nation acting unilaterally, indifferent to the concerns of the broader international community.

Balancing national autonomy and international cooperation becomes a diplomatic tightrope. While asserting one's interests is a legitimate aspect of foreign policy, the challenge lies in doing so while maintaining respect for the diverse opinions and needs of a multipolar world.

3. The Perception Puzzle: Crafting a Diplomatic Narrative

Perceptions matter, and how a nation crafts its diplomatic narrative influences its standing on the global stage. The perception of arrogance or indifference to international opinions can impact not only diplomatic relations but also public sentiment worldwide.

Engaging in transparent and inclusive decision-making processes can counter perceptions of disregard. Actively seeking input, collaborating with international partners, and demonstrating a commitment to shared global goals contribute to a narrative of responsible global leadership.

Diplomacy is not just about policy but also about communication. Crafting a diplomatic narrative that emphasizes collaboration, openness, and a willingness to listen can recalibrate perceptions. It's a call for a diplomatic approach that resonates with the ideals of partnership and cooperation.

4. The Multilateral Imperative: A Diplomatic Antidote

One potent antidote to critiques of unilateral decision-making and perceived disregard for international opinions is embracing multilateralism. Engaging with international institutions, seeking consensus on critical issues, and fostering a culture of collaboration can reshape the narrative surrounding a nation's diplomatic approach.

Multilateral approaches not only provide avenues for diverse perspectives but also enhance the legitimacy of decisions. Working through international forums and respecting the principles of international law can strengthen diplomatic relations and reinforce a commitment to global cooperation.

The challenge lies in recognizing the benefits of shared decision-making and the richness that diverse viewpoints bring to the table. Multilateralism is not just a diplomatic strategy but a reflection of a nation's recognition of its interconnectedness with the broader global community.

5. Soft Diplomacy: Bridging Gaps with Cultural Sensitivity

Soft diplomacy, the art of building relationships through culture, education, and public engagement, offers a nuanced approach to counter perceptions of disregard. It involves fostering understanding and goodwill on a people-to-people level, recognizing the cultural tapestry that enriches global relations.

Cultural sensitivity becomes a key component of soft diplomacy. Engaging with diverse cultures, acknowledging the value of different perspectives, and promoting cultural exchange programs contribute to a narrative that transcends political differences.

The influence of American pop culture and educational institutions can be powerful tools for soft diplomacy. Leveraging these cultural elements with a keen awareness of local nuances can bridge gaps and foster connections that transcend political disagreements.

Navigating the Diplomatic Maze

As we conclude our exploration of unilateral decision-making and the perception of disregard for international opinions, the complexities of navigating the diplomatic maze become evident. Diplomacy is not just about asserting power but about building relationships, understanding diverse perspectives, and crafting a narrative that resonates with the ideals of cooperation.

Chapter 7: Global Power Dynamics: Navigating the Shadows of Superpower Resentment

In the complex landscape of global affairs, the United States stands as a towering presence, a superpower with unparalleled influence across economic, military, and cultural domains. Yet, with great power comes great scrutiny, and this chapter delves into the nuances of the fear and resentment that can emanate from the United States' status as a global superpower.

1. The Burden of Power: Balancing Act of a Superpower

As the world's preeminent superpower, the United States wields influence that extends far beyond its borders. This influence, however, is a double-edged sword, as it can evoke admiration and collaboration but also instigate fear and resentment. The burden of power requires a delicate balance between asserting national interests and fostering cooperation on the global stage.

One aspect contributing to the perception of superpower arrogance is the notion of exceptionalism, the belief that the U.S. holds a unique and irreplaceable role in the world. While rooted in a sense of national pride, exceptionalism can be perceived as a form of entitlement that breeds resentment among nations with different histories, cultures, and aspirations.

2. The Fear of Hegemony: A Looming Shadow

Fear of hegemony, the dominance or control of one state over others, looms as a shadow in the global consciousness. As the world's superpower, the U.S. has the capability to shape international events and influence the trajectories of nations. However, this very capability can evoke fear among other nations, sparking concerns about the imposition of values, interests, and ideologies.

Historical precedents, such as the Cold War era, where the U.S. and the Soviet Union competed for global dominance, contribute to the perception of great powers engaging in strategic rivalries. The fear of a unipolar world, where a single superpower dictates the rules, fuels concerns about the erosion of national autonomy and the potential for exploitation.

3. Economic Influence: The Unequal Power Play

Economic power, a cornerstone of U.S. influence, also plays a role in shaping global power dynamics. The dominance of the U.S. dollar, the influence of American multinational corporations, and the impact of economic policies on the global market contribute to perceptions of an unequal power play.

Trade policies, sanctions, and economic partnerships can be viewed through the lens of economic imperialism, where the interests of the superpower take precedence over the concerns of smaller or less economically robust nations.

The fear of economic coercion and dependence on U.S. markets becomes a source of resentment, challenging the ideals of fair and equitable international trade.

4. Military Might: The Sword of Superpower Influence

The United States' military prowess is a defining aspect of its superpower status. While military strength can be a stabilizing force, it also raises concerns about the potential for intervention, coercion, and the assertion of dominance. Military interventions, justified or not, contribute to a narrative of a superpower acting as a global arbiter.

The fear of military hegemony is amplified by the capacity for intervention in regions far from the U.S. homeland. Military bases, strategic alliances, and the projection of force contribute to the perception of a global garrison, evoking concerns about the erosion of national sovereignty and the potential for interventions that prioritize the interests of the superpower.

5. Cultural Imperialism: The Soft Power Conundrum

While soft power, the ability to shape preferences through culture and ideology, is a significant asset for the U.S., it also becomes a source of apprehension. Cultural imperialism, the dominance of American cultural products and values, can lead to fears of homogenization and the erosion of local traditions.

The global spread of American movies, music, and technology contributes to the perception that cultural diversity is being supplanted by a singular narrative. The fear of losing cultural identity and the potential for a global monoculture fuel sentiments of resentment, challenging the notion that cultural influence should be a force for mutual enrichment.

6. Diplomatic Dilemmas: Striking a Balance

In the realm of diplomacy, the actions and decisions of a superpower carry weight that can shape the course of international relations. Striking a balance between asserting influence and respecting the agency of other nations is a diplomatic dilemma that requires finesse.

Diplomatic actions, whether through alliances, negotiations, or international agreements, can either assuage fears of hegemony or exacerbate them. The challenge lies in cultivating a diplomatic approach that fosters cooperation, recognizes diverse perspectives, and acknowledges the aspirations of nations beyond the superpower's orbit.

7. The Call for Empathy: Understanding Global Perspectives

Addressing the fear and resentment stemming from superpower status requires a nuanced understanding of global perspectives. Empathy becomes a crucial element in acknowledging the concerns and aspirations of nations that may feel overshadowed by the superpower's influence.

Engaging in genuine dialogue, actively listening to the grievances of other nations, and demonstrating a commitment to collaborative solutions can reshape the narrative surrounding superpower influence. The call for empathy is a recognition that power dynamics should be tempered with an understanding of the complex realities that define the global landscape.

Navigating the Shadows

As we conclude our exploration of the fear and resentment stemming from the U.S. as a global superpower, we recognize the intricate shadows that accompany great power. The narrative is one of complexity, where the actions and influence of a superpower are scrutinized in the global spotlight.

Navigating the Web of Power: Understanding How Dynamics Shape Global Relationships

In the vast tapestry of global relations, the dynamics of power play a central role in shaping interactions, alliances, and conflicts. This chapter aims to unravel the intricacies of how power dynamics influence international relationships, providing a reader-friendly exploration of the forces that define the ebb and flow of diplomacy on the world stage.

1. The Chessboard of Nations: Power as a Driving Force

Imagine the world as a grand chessboard, where nations are the pieces and power is the force propelling the game forward. Power, in the realm of international relations, is multifaceted, encompassing economic, military, diplomatic, and cultural dimensions. The distribution and balance of this power among nations define the dynamics that govern their relationships.

The great powers, often referred to as the "big players" on the geopolitical stage, wield influence that extends far beyond their borders. Their actions, decisions, and policies create ripples that shape the course of global affairs. Understanding how this power is wielded and perceived is essential to decoding the complex dance of international relationships.

2. Economic Leverage: The Currency of Influence

Economic power stands as a cornerstone in the edifice of global influence. Nations with robust economies can leverage their financial strength to shape international trade, investment, and development. The rise of economic blocs and partnerships reflects the recognition that economic collaboration is a potent tool for advancing national interests.

Consider the economic ties between the United States and China. As two economic giants, their relationship is not merely bilateral; it influences global markets, trade routes, and the stability of the international financial system. Economic power dynamics manifest not only in wealth but also in the ability to set the rules of the economic game.

3. Military Might: The Sword and Shield of Nations

Military power, the ability to defend one's interests and project force, is a fundamental aspect of global power dynamics. Nations with formidable military capabilities not only secure their borders but also assert influence in regions far from home. The presence of military bases, strategic alliances, and the possession of advanced weaponry become symbols of a nation's military prowess.

The United States, as a superpower, maintains a global military presence. Its alliances with NATO member countries, military bases in key regions, and technological superiority contribute to a perception of military dominance. The influence of military power extends beyond conflicts; it shapes the strategic calculations and decision-making of nations across the globe.

4. Diplomacy and Soft Power: The Art of Persuasion

Diplomacy, often described as the art of negotiation and compromise, is a subtle yet powerful tool in the realm of international relations. Diplomatic influence goes beyond the blunt force of military or economic power; it involves the finesse of building relationships, brokering agreements, and navigating the complexities of a diverse world.

Soft power, a concept coined by political scientist Joseph Nye, refers to the ability to shape preferences through appeal and attraction. Cultural influence, diplomatic finesse, and the ability to inspire admiration contribute to a nation's soft power. The United States, with its global cultural impact through Hollywood, technology, and educational institutions, exemplifies the potential of soft power in shaping international perceptions.

5. Alliance Building: Strengthening Positions through Unity

In the grand tapestry of global power dynamics, alliances emerge as crucial threads that bind nations together. The formation of alliances reflects a recognition that collective strength is often more potent than individual prowess. NATO, the European Union, and regional partnerships exemplify the strategic calculus of nations seeking to strengthen their positions through unity.

Alliances not only provide a platform for collective defense but also serve as forums for diplomatic collaboration. Shared values, common interests, and mutual security concerns become the adhesive that binds nations in alliances. Understanding the dynamics of alliance-building is key to deciphering the complexities of global relationships.

6. The Role of Asymmetry: Navigating Power Disparities

While power dynamics often involve nations on relatively equal footing, the reality is that vast disparities exist among countries. Asymmetric power relationships, where one nation significantly outweighs another in terms of resources or capabilities, introduce complexities that influence international interactions.

Consider the relationship between a superpower and a smaller, less influential nation. The power asymmetry can lead to challenges in diplomacy, economic negotiations, and even cultural exchanges. Navigating these disparities requires a nuanced understanding of how power imbalances shape the behaviors and expectations of nations in the global arena.

7. The Shifting Sands: Adapting to Dynamic Power Realities

The dynamics of power are not static; they evolve in response to geopolitical shifts, economic trends, and cultural transformations. The rise of new powers, changes in global economic structures, and the emergence of unconventional threats reshape the power landscape. Nations must adapt to these dynamic realities to navigate the currents of international relationships effectively.

China's ascent as a global economic powerhouse, for instance, has altered the dynamics of power in East Asia and beyond. The response of other nations, the recalibration of alliances, and the adjustments in economic strategies exemplify how the shifting sands of power influence the behavior of nations on the global stage.

Decoding the Language of Power

As we conclude our exploration of how power dynamics influence international relationships, we recognize that the language of power is complex and multifaceted. Nations engage in a constant dance, juggling economic interests, military capabilities, diplomatic finesse, and the intangible allure of soft power.

Chapter 8: Religious and Social Issues - Understanding Anti-US Sentiments

In the intricate tapestry of global relations, religious and social factors play a significant role in shaping perspectives and fostering either understanding or resentment. As we delve into the realm of anti-American sentiments, it becomes crucial to explore the intricate ways in which religious and social differences contribute to the nuanced landscape of global opinion.

The Melting Pot: Diversity or Discord?
America is often referred to as a "melting pot," a metaphor that encapsulates its rich tapestry of diverse cultures, ethnicities, and religions. While this cultural diversity is touted as a source of strength, it can also be a breeding ground for misunderstanding and tension.

Religious pluralism in the United States is undeniable, with a plethora of faiths coexisting within its borders. From Christianity and Islam to Hinduism and Buddhism, the nation is home to a multitude of religious traditions. However, the very diversity that is celebrated domestically can contribute to suspicion and skepticism abroad.

In certain instances, American policies are viewed through the lens of religious affiliations. The perceived alignment of the U.S. with particular religious groups, either at home or abroad, can generate anti-American sentiments among those who feel marginalized or opposed to those groups.

Understanding this intricate interplay between foreign policy, domestic religious dynamics, and global perceptions is crucial in deciphering the roots of anti-U.S. sentiment.

Social Dynamics: A Tale of Inequality
Beyond religious diversity, the social fabric of the United States is woven with threads of economic disparity, racial tension, and social inequality. While these issues are not exclusive to the U.S., they do contribute to a perception of hypocrisy when contrasted with the nation's global image as a beacon of freedom and equality.

Critics argue that the American Dream, often portrayed as the pinnacle of success through hard work and determination, is not equally accessible to all. Socioeconomic disparities and racial inequalities persist, breeding resentment among those who feel left behind or marginalized by the system.

This sense of inequity is magnified on the global stage, with anti-American sentiments fueled by perceptions of cultural imperialism and neocolonialism. The exportation of American culture through media, technology, and consumerism can be seen as an imposition on traditional values and social structures in other nations, leading to resistance and animosity.

Clash of Values: Balancing Individualism and Collectivism
The American emphasis on individualism and personal freedoms, while celebrated within the nation, can be a source of friction when viewed from a more collectivist cultural perspective.

In many societies, the emphasis is placed on the collective good and communal harmony rather than individual rights.

This clash of values is exemplified in debates over issues such as freedom of speech, LGBTQ+ rights, and the role of government in individual lives. While these debates are intrinsic to American society, they can be viewed with skepticism or even disdain by cultures that prioritize communal well-being over individual autonomy.

Understanding and addressing these differences in values are essential in bridging the gap between the United States and those who harbor anti-American sentiments. Recognizing the validity of diverse cultural perspectives and finding common ground based on shared human values can foster greater understanding and cooperation on the global stage.

The Role of Social Media: Amplifying Divides
In the age of instant communication, social media plays a pivotal role in shaping perceptions and disseminating information. Unfortunately, it can also be a breeding ground for misinformation and the amplification of negative sentiments.

Incidents that may be isolated or unrepresentative of the broader American society can be magnified and distorted through the lens of social media, contributing to a skewed global perception. It is crucial to recognize the impact of these platforms on shaping opinions and work towards fostering a more nuanced understanding of the complexities within American society.

Religious and social differences are integral components of the complex tapestry that forms global perspectives on the United States. By acknowledging and addressing these differences with empathy and understanding, the U.S. can strive to build bridges rather than walls, fostering a world where diverse cultures can coexist in harmony. As we continue our exploration, the next section will delve into the cultural clashes related to values and beliefs, unraveling the intricate web that contributes to anti-American sentiments.

Cultural Clashes - Unraveling Values and Beliefs
In the mosaic of global interactions, cultural clashes play a pivotal role in shaping perceptions and fueling sentiments. As we continue our exploration of anti-American sentiments, we turn our attention to the intricate web of cultural clashes, where values and beliefs intertwine, sometimes harmoniously, but often with discord.

The American Dream vs. Local Realities
The concept of the "American Dream" has long been a symbol of hope and aspiration, promising a better life through hard work and determination. However, the global perception of this dream can vary significantly, leading to clashes in expectations.

In some regions, the American Dream may be seen as an inspiring beacon, while in others, it might be criticized as an unattainable illusion. Cultural differences in attitudes toward success, wealth, and social mobility contribute to these clashes, shaping how the American Dream is perceived and, subsequently, influencing anti-American sentiments.

Cultural Imperialism: Exporting Values or Imposing Ideals?
The global influence of American media, technology, and popular culture is undeniable. However, this influence is a double-edged sword, as it can be seen both as a form of cultural exchange and as a means of imposing American values on diverse societies.

Critics argue that the dominance of Hollywood, fast food chains, and multinational corporations contributes to a homogenization of cultures, eroding local traditions and values. This perception of cultural imperialism can lead to resentment and anti-American sentiments, as communities strive to preserve their unique identities against what they perceive as an encroachment of foreign ideals.

Freedom of Speech: A Global Dilemma
While freedom of speech is a cornerstone of American democracy, its interpretation and application can be a source of contention on the global stage. Issues such as hate speech, blasphemy, and political dissent may be approached differently in various cultures, leading to clashes in expectations regarding the boundaries of expression.

Instances where American individuals or entities exercise their right to free speech may be perceived as offensive or disrespectful in other cultural contexts. Understanding these differing perspectives on freedom of expression is crucial in navigating the complexities of international relations and mitigating anti-American sentiments stemming from cultural misunderstandings.

Gender Roles and Equality: A Cultural Divide
The evolving landscape of gender roles and equality in the United States reflects progress and ongoing debates within American society. However, cultural differences in perceptions of gender roles can lead to misunderstandings and contribute to anti-American sentiments.

While strides have been made towards gender equality in the U.S., certain cultural contexts may view these changes as a departure from traditional values. Bridging this cultural divide requires a nuanced understanding of diverse perspectives on gender roles, acknowledging the progress made in the U.S. while respecting the autonomy of other cultures to define their societal norms.

Environmental Stewardship: A Global Responsibility
The U.S.'s approach to environmental issues can be a point of contention on the global stage. While there is growing awareness of environmental challenges, differing perspectives on the urgency of addressing these issues and the appropriate measures to take can lead to cultural clashes.

Some may view the U.S. as a proponent of unsustainable consumption patterns and environmental policies, contributing to global challenges. Bridging this gap requires open dialogue and collaboration to find common ground on shared environmental responsibilities while respecting cultural nuances.

Navigating Cultural Clashes: Toward Mutual Understanding

Understanding and addressing cultural clashes related to values and beliefs are essential steps in fostering positive global relations. It involves acknowledging diverse perspectives, engaging in open dialogue, and cultivating a sense of shared humanity. By recognizing the complexity of cultural dynamics, the United States can work towards building bridges and promoting a more inclusive and empathetic world.

Chapter 9: Media Influence and Propaganda - Shaping Perceptions of the U.S.

In the age of information, media plays a paramount role in shaping public perceptions and influencing the way nations are viewed globally. As we navigate the intricacies of anti-American sentiments, it's essential to delve into the powerful impact of media portrayal and the dynamics that mold the lenses through which the world sees the United States.

The Power of Narratives: Shaping Global Perspectives
Media, in its various forms, weaves narratives that transcend borders, influencing how people perceive distant nations and their actions. The United States, as a global powerhouse, is both a subject and an object of media attention. The portrayal of the U.S. in news, entertainment, and social media significantly contributes to the formation of opinions worldwide.

News Media: Framing Reality
News outlets, both domestic and international, play a pivotal role in disseminating information about the United States. The framing of news stories, selection of headlines, and the tone of reporting all contribute to the narrative that is presented to the global audience.

Perceptions of bias in news reporting can fuel anti-American sentiments, with some accusing media outlets of presenting a skewed or incomplete picture of events. It is crucial for consumers of news to be aware of potential biases and seek diverse sources to form a more comprehensive understanding of U.S. actions and policies.

Entertainment Media: Hollywood's Global Impact
Hollywood, with its vast influence, has become a cultural ambassador for the United States. The movies and television shows produced in Hollywood shape not only American culture but also contribute significantly to how the U.S. is perceived worldwide.

While American entertainment is beloved globally, it can also be a source of criticism. Accusations of cultural appropriation, stereotyping, and the perpetuation of certain narratives can lead to negative perceptions. Understanding the impact of entertainment media on global attitudes allows for a more nuanced interpretation of the relationship between cultural exports and international sentiment.

Social Media: The Amplification Effect
In the digital age, social media platforms serve as a global town square, where ideas, images, and narratives circulate at an unprecedented speed. The influence of social media in shaping perceptions of the United States cannot be overstated.

Viral content, whether accurate or not, can shape public opinion and contribute to the amplification of anti-American sentiments. The rapid spread of information on social media requires a discerning audience that critically evaluates sources and considers multiple perspectives to avoid falling prey to misinformation.

The Dynamics of Soft Power: Winning Hearts and Minds
Soft power, the ability to influence through attraction and persuasion rather than coercion, is a key aspect of international relations. Media portrayal is a central component of soft power, and the United States has long recognized its potential to shape global attitudes.

Public diplomacy efforts, such as cultural exchanges, educational programs, and international broadcasting, are designed to present the U.S. in a positive light. However, the success of these initiatives depends on the receptivity of the global audience and the alignment of portrayed values with local perspectives.

The Dark Side: Propaganda and Manipulation
As we navigate the complex landscape of media influence, it's essential to address the darker side of information dissemination—propaganda. Propaganda, whether state-sponsored or disseminated by non-state actors, seeks to manipulate perceptions, often by presenting a biased or distorted view of reality.

State-Sponsored Propaganda: A Weapon of Influence
Some nations employ state-sponsored propaganda to advance their geopolitical interests and shape global narratives. Anti-American propaganda may be used as a tool to rally domestic support, divert attention from internal issues, or undermine U.S. credibility on the world stage.

Understanding the existence and impact of state-sponsored propaganda is crucial in deciphering the complex web of information that shapes global attitudes toward the United States. It necessitates a critical examination of sources and an awareness of the geopolitical motivations that may underpin certain narratives.

Non-State Actors: Navigating Information Warfare
In the digital age, non-state actors, including extremist groups and hacktivist collectives, engage in information warfare to promote their agendas. Anti-American sentiment can be fueled by targeted disinformation campaigns that exploit existing grievances and amplify divisive narratives.

Addressing the influence of non-state actors requires a concerted effort in cybersecurity, media literacy education, and international cooperation. By strengthening defenses against information warfare, nations can mitigate the impact of propaganda on global perceptions.

Navigating the Information Landscape
Media influence and propaganda wield significant power in shaping perceptions of the United States on the global stage. As consumers of information, it is incumbent upon individuals to approach media narratives with critical thinking, seeking diverse sources and perspectives to form a more nuanced understanding of the complex realities that define international relations.

The Role of Propaganda - Unmasking the Shadows
In the vast arena of global influence, propaganda emerges as a powerful force that can mold perceptions, ignite emotions, and foster sentiments, including anti-Americanism. As we embark on this exploration of the shadows, it is crucial to unravel the intricate mechanisms through which propaganda influences anti-American sentiment.

Understanding Propaganda: A Primer
Propaganda, in its essence, is the strategic dissemination of information designed to shape public opinion and influence behavior. While the term often carries a negative connotation, it is essential to recognize that propaganda can manifest in various forms, ranging from overt state-sponsored campaigns to subtle messaging embedded in popular culture.

In the context of anti-American sentiment, propaganda can be a tool wielded by both state and non-state actors. Its objectives may include tarnishing the image of the United States, sowing discord, and advancing specific agendas. Let's delve into the multifaceted ways in which propaganda operates on the global stage.

State-Sponsored Propaganda: Shaping Narratives for Geopolitical Ends

States, driven by geopolitical interests, frequently engage in the art of state-sponsored propaganda. The objective is clear: to influence international opinion in a manner that aligns with their strategic goals. Anti-American propaganda, emanating from various corners of the globe, often serves as a means to advance political narratives.

1. Shaping the Enemy Image: In the theater of international relations, creating a negative image of an adversary is a common tactic. Anti-American propaganda may depict the U.S. as an imperialistic power, highlighting instances of perceived aggression or intervention in other nations.

2. Diverting Attention: State-sponsored propaganda can serve as a diversionary tactic, deflecting attention from internal issues by focusing on perceived flaws or controversies related to the United States. By directing public discourse toward external matters, governments may mitigate scrutiny of their own shortcomings.

3. Undermining Credibility: Propaganda aims to erode the credibility of the United States on the global stage. Accusations of hypocrisy, human rights violations, or double standards in foreign policy can be amplified to fuel skepticism and distrust.

Non-State Actors: Harnessing Information Warfare

In the digital age, non-state actors wield unprecedented power in the realm of information warfare. Extremist groups, hacktivist collectives, and ideological movements leverage propaganda to amplify their messages and garner support for their causes.

1. Exploiting Grievances: Anti-American propaganda by non-state actors often exploits existing grievances, whether rooted in geopolitical conflicts, economic disparities, or cultural clashes. By tapping into these grievances, propagandists can mobilize support against the perceived common enemy.

2. Disinformation Campaigns: Disinformation, the intentional spread of false or misleading information, is a potent weapon in the arsenal of non-state actors. Fabricated narratives, conspiracy theories, and manipulated visuals can contribute to a distorted perception of the United States, fostering mistrust and hostility.

3. Social Media Amplification: The ubiquity of social media provides a fertile ground for the dissemination of propaganda. Non-state actors leverage platforms to amplify their messages, reaching a global audience with unprecedented speed. Hashtag campaigns, viral videos, and coordinated online activities contribute to the amplification of anti-American sentiments.

Cultural Sensitivity: Propaganda Tailored to Local Contexts

Effective propaganda understands the nuances of cultural contexts and tailors messages to resonate with target audiences. Anti-American propaganda often takes advantage of cultural sensitivities, framing narratives in ways that align with local values, beliefs, and historical grievances.

1. Cultural Appropriation: Propagandists may appropriate symbols, narratives, or historical events familiar to the target audience, framing them in a manner that supports the anti-American narrative. This form of cultural manipulation reinforces the idea that the United States is an external threat to local values.

2. Framing Ideological Clashes: Propaganda often frames conflicts as ideological struggles, emphasizing perceived clashes of values and beliefs. By framing the U.S. as antithetical to local ideologies, propagandists seek to deepen existing fault lines and foster a sense of opposition.

Countering Propaganda: Building Resilience and Media Literacy

As we confront the pervasive influence of propaganda, it is imperative to explore strategies for countering its impact and building resilience against manipulation.

1. Media Literacy Education: Empowering individuals with the skills to critically evaluate information sources is a crucial step in countering propaganda. Media literacy education equips people to discern between reliable and biased information, fostering a more discerning and informed public.

2. International Cooperation: Propaganda often transcends national borders, making international cooperation essential. Collaborative efforts to share information, counter disinformation, and promote fact-checking initiatives can strengthen global defenses against the manipulation of public opinion.

3. Responsible Media Practices: Media outlets play a pivotal role in shaping narratives. Encouraging responsible journalism practices, fact-checking, and maintaining editorial integrity are essential in countering the influence of propaganda. Media organizations can serve as bulwarks against misinformation by prioritizing accuracy and impartiality.

Navigating the Propaganda Landscape
In the complex landscape of global influence, propaganda emerges as a formidable force, shaping perceptions and fueling sentiments. Understanding the tactics employed by state and non-state actors is essential for individuals, societies, and nations to navigate the propaganda landscape effectively.

Chapter 10: Misunderstandings and Stereotypes - Bridging the Divide

In the intricate tapestry of global perceptions, misunderstandings and stereotypes often cast shadows over the nuanced realities that define the United States. As we venture into the heart of anti-American sentiments, it is imperative to unravel the common misconceptions and stereotypes that contribute to the chasm between nations.

Myth 1: The Monolithic America

One pervasive misconception is the tendency to view America as a monolithic entity, neglecting the rich diversity that defines the nation. The United States is a mosaic of cultures, ethnicities, and traditions, with each region contributing to a multifaceted national identity. Stereotyping the entire nation based on certain characteristics or behaviors oversimplifies the complexity of American society.

Reality: America's strength lies in its diversity. From the urban landscapes of New York City to the rural expanses of the Midwest, each region offers a unique perspective, contributing to the vibrant tapestry of American life.

Myth 2: The Hollywood Illusion

Hollywood, with its glamorous portrayal of life and culture, often becomes a lens through which the world perceives the United States. However, mistaking Hollywood narratives for an accurate representation of American life can lead to skewed impressions.

Reality: Hollywood is a creative industry that crafts stories for entertainment. While it reflects certain aspects of American culture, it doesn't capture the full spectrum of everyday life, values, and experiences across the nation.

Myth 3: The Land of Instant Success
The American Dream, while emblematic of aspiration and opportunity, is sometimes misconstrued as a promise of instant success. This misconception can lead to misunderstandings about the challenges and hard work required to achieve one's goals in the United States.

Reality: The American Dream emphasizes opportunity and upward mobility, but success often comes through perseverance, dedication, and hard work. It is a journey, not an immediate destination.

Myth 4: The Cultural Ignorance
Another stereotype involves viewing Americans as culturally ignorant or indifferent to global affairs. This misconception oversimplifies the diverse interests, global awareness, and engagement of Americans in international issues.

Reality: Many Americans are actively involved in global affairs, and there is a rich tapestry of individuals who are passionate about learning, understanding, and contributing to global conversations.

Myth 5: The Obesity Epidemic
The stereotype of Americans as a uniformly overweight population is not only inaccurate but also perpetuates harmful biases. While obesity is a health concern in the U.S., generalizing the entire population based on this stereotype oversimplifies the complex factors contributing to health and wellness.

Reality: Health and lifestyle choices vary widely among Americans. It's important to recognize individual agency and the multifaceted factors influencing health outcomes.

Myth 6: The Gun Culture
The perception of the U.S. as a nation obsessed with guns is a stereotype rooted in media portrayals and specific incidents. While gun ownership is a complex and debated issue, it doesn't define the entirety of American society.

Reality: Gun ownership is a constitutional right, but views on this issue vary widely across the country. It's essential to engage in nuanced discussions rather than relying on broad stereotypes.

Myth 7: The Economic Divide
The stereotype of America as a land of extreme wealth and poverty oversimplifies the economic realities. While economic inequality is a concern, it doesn't encapsulate the entirety of the U.S. economy or the experiences of its diverse population.

Reality: America has a complex economic landscape, with a broad spectrum of wealth and opportunities. Understanding this complexity is crucial for accurate perceptions.

Addressing Stereotypes: A Call for Nuance
Challenging these stereotypes requires a nuanced understanding of the United States, acknowledging its diversity and embracing the complexities that define the nation. By dispelling misconceptions, we pave the way for constructive dialogue and foster a more accurate global understanding of America.

Strategies for Bridging the Divide
As we strive to bridge the gap between perceptions and reality, it is essential to cultivate efforts that foster understanding and dispel stereotypes. Here are key strategies to bridge cultural gaps and promote mutual understanding:

1. Cultural Exchange Programs
Promoting cultural exchange programs facilitates direct interaction between individuals from different nations. These programs offer a firsthand experience of diverse cultures, dispelling stereotypes and fostering genuine connections.

2. Media Literacy Education
Equipping individuals with media literacy skills empowers them to critically evaluate information sources. By understanding how media narratives are constructed, people can navigate through stereotypes and form more informed opinions.

3. Dialogues and Forums
Creating spaces for open dialogue and forums allows individuals to share perspectives, challenge stereotypes, and build bridges of understanding. Constructive conversations help break down barriers and promote empathy.

4. Travel and Tourism
Traveling provides an opportunity to experience different cultures firsthand. By exploring diverse regions within the U.S., as well as engaging with local communities, individuals gain a more nuanced understanding of American life beyond stereotypes.

5. Education Initiatives
Integrating global perspectives into educational curricula fosters a more comprehensive understanding of different cultures. Education initiatives that emphasize cultural diversity and inclusivity contribute to breaking down stereotypes from an early age.

6. Collaborative Projects
Encouraging collaborative projects across borders, whether in the arts, sciences, or technology, creates opportunities for shared experiences and mutual learning. Collaborative endeavors emphasize commonalities and shared goals.

Navigating Towards Understanding
In our exploration of anti-American sentiments, dispelling stereotypes and addressing misunderstandings emerge as essential steps toward fostering mutual understanding. By embracing the complexity and diversity of the United States, we move beyond simplistic narratives, paving the way for a more interconnected and empathetic global community.

As we embark on the final chapter of our journey, we will explore the efforts and initiatives undertaken to bridge cultural gaps and foster understanding between nations. Join us in discovering the pathways that lead towards a world built on cooperation, empathy, and shared humanity.

Bridging Cultural Gaps - Fostering Global Understanding
In the realm of international relations, the importance of bridging cultural gaps and fostering understanding cannot be overstated. As we conclude our exploration of anti-American sentiments, this chapter focuses on the tireless efforts and initiatives aimed at building connections, dismantling stereotypes, and promoting a world where diverse cultures coexist harmoniously.

Cultural Exchange Programs: Building Bridges Across Borders
Cultural exchange programs stand as beacons of mutual understanding, providing individuals with the opportunity to immerse themselves in different cultures. These initiatives facilitate firsthand experiences, enabling participants to challenge preconceived notions and build genuine connections.

Whether through student exchanges, artist residencies, or professional programs, these exchanges promote empathy, dispel stereotypes, and contribute to the formation of a global community based on shared experiences.

Media Literacy Education: Navigating the Information Landscape
In an era dominated by information overload, media literacy education emerges as a crucial tool for empowering individuals to navigate the complex information landscape. By teaching critical thinking skills and encouraging a discerning approach to media consumption, education initiatives aim to counteract the influence of misinformation and stereotypes.

Efforts to integrate media literacy into school curricula, community programs, and online platforms empower individuals to question narratives, recognize bias, and contribute to a more informed and interconnected global society.

Dialogues and Forums: Spaces for Open Conversation
Open dialogues and forums serve as catalysts for meaningful conversations, providing spaces where individuals from diverse backgrounds can share their perspectives, challenge stereotypes, and find common ground. These platforms foster understanding by creating an environment where people can listen, learn, and engage in constructive discussions.

International forums, community dialogues, and online platforms enable individuals to voice their experiences, contributing to the dismantling of stereotypes and the cultivation of a global perspective that values diversity.

Travel and Tourism: Exploring the Tapestry of Cultures
Traveling offers a profound way to bridge cultural gaps, providing individuals with the opportunity to immerse themselves in different environments, traditions, and ways of life. Tourism initiatives that encourage responsible and respectful exploration contribute to a deeper understanding of diverse cultures.

As people engage with local communities, savor unique cuisines, and witness cultural practices firsthand, they develop a nuanced appreciation for the intricacies that define a culture, transcending the limitations of stereotypes.

Education Initiatives: Nurturing Inclusivity from an Early Age
Education initiatives play a pivotal role in nurturing inclusivity and understanding from an early age. By incorporating global perspectives, cultural diversity, and empathy into educational curricula, institutions help shape future generations with a more nuanced understanding of the world.

Programs that promote cultural awareness, inclusivity, and the celebration of diversity create a foundation for building a society that values and respects differences.

Collaborative Projects: Uniting Across Borders
Collaborative projects across borders exemplify the potential for shared endeavors to foster understanding. Whether in the fields of science, arts, or technology, joint projects emphasize common goals and shared humanity, transcending cultural differences.

By working together on global challenges or creative endeavors, individuals from diverse backgrounds build connections, learn from one another, and contribute to a world where collaboration prevails over division.

Grassroots Initiatives: Community-Led Change
At the heart of fostering cultural understanding are grassroots initiatives driven by communities themselves. Local efforts to promote inclusivity, celebrate cultural diversity, and create spaces for cross-cultural interactions are instrumental in building bridges on a micro level.

Community-led events, cultural festivals, and grassroots movements contribute to a sense of belonging, dispelling stereotypes, and nurturing an environment where diversity is celebrated.

Towards a Connected World
Efforts to bridge cultural gaps and foster understanding are vital components of a global society that thrives on cooperation, empathy, and shared humanity. As we conclude our journey through the intricacies of anti-American sentiments, it becomes evident that building connections across borders is not only a pursuit but a necessity.

By embracing cultural exchange, promoting media literacy, encouraging open dialogue, and supporting collaborative projects, we pave the way towards a world where diverse cultures coalesce, enriching the global narrative with a tapestry of perspectives. In the spirit of mutual understanding, let us strive for a future where stereotypes are dismantled, and the bridges we build today become the foundations of a more interconnected and harmonious world.

Conclusion: Nurturing Understanding for a Harmonious World

In our exploration of anti-American sentiments, we've traversed the intricate landscapes of geopolitics, cultural dynamics, media influence, and the power of perception. As we conclude this journey, let's distill the key findings that have emerged from our exploration and reflect on the imperative of understanding global perspectives.

Summarizing Key Findings
Complexity of Global Relations: The nuances of global relations reveal that perceptions of the United States are shaped by a myriad of factors, including historical events, cultural dynamics, and geopolitical considerations.

Media's Pivotal Role: Media, in its various forms, plays a central role in influencing opinions and shaping narratives. The power of media, both in reflecting and constructing reality, highlights the need for media literacy and critical engagement.

Impact of Stereotypes: Stereotypes and misconceptions, often rooted in media portrayals and cultural misunderstandings, contribute significantly to anti-American sentiments. Dispelling these stereotypes is crucial for fostering accurate global perceptions.

Cultural Exchange and Understanding: Initiatives such as cultural exchange programs, media literacy education, dialogues, and collaborative projects emerge as powerful tools in building bridges, dispelling stereotypes, and fostering genuine understanding.

The Importance of Understanding Global Perspectives
Understanding global perspectives is not merely an academic pursuit but a cornerstone of a harmonious and interconnected world. As our societies become more interconnected and interdependent, the repercussions of misunderstandings and misperceptions ripple across borders.

Promoting Peace and Stability: A nuanced understanding of global perspectives is essential for promoting peace and stability. By appreciating diverse viewpoints, nations can build diplomatic bridges and navigate international relations with empathy.

Addressing Global Challenges: Global challenges, from climate change to pandemics, require collaborative solutions. Understanding different perspectives enables nations to work together effectively, pooling resources and expertise for the greater good.

Fostering Inclusive Societies: Cultivating an understanding of global perspectives contributes to the creation of inclusive societies that celebrate diversity. Embracing cultural differences strengthens social cohesion and enriches the fabric of communities.

Calls for Diplomatic Efforts, Dialogue, and Mutual Understanding
In light of our exploration, it is clear that fostering mutual understanding is not only an aspiration but an imperative. The following calls to action emerge:

Diplomatic Engagement: Nations must prioritize diplomatic efforts as a means of resolving conflicts, building alliances, and fostering cooperation. Open channels of communication lay the foundation for constructive dialogue.

Facilitating Dialogue: International forums, dialogues, and platforms for open conversation should be actively facilitated. These spaces provide opportunities for nations to discuss differences, share perspectives, and find common ground.

Promoting Cultural Diplomacy: Cultural diplomacy, through initiatives like cultural exchanges and collaborative projects, can be a potent force in building bridges between nations. By showcasing the richness of diverse cultures, nations can forge connections that transcend political differences.

Investing in Education: Education is a powerful tool for nurturing global understanding. Curricula that incorporate global perspectives, cultural literacy, and critical thinking skills contribute to a generation that values diversity and strives for unity.

As we embark on the path forward, let us heed the lessons learned from our exploration and actively contribute to a world where diplomacy, dialogue, and mutual understanding are the guiding principles. In embracing the complexity of global relations, we pave the way for a future where nations collaborate harmoniously, driven by a shared vision of a more interconnected and compassionate world.

It's important to note that sentiments toward the United States can vary widely within countries and are influenced by numerous factors, including political, economic, cultural, and historical considerations. Below are only some of the countries where anti-U.S. sentiments have been reported and common reasons often cited:

Iran:

Reasons: Historical events, such as the CIA-backed coup in 1953, the Iran-Iraq War, and ongoing geopolitical tensions, contribute to anti-U.S. sentiments. The U.S. withdrawal from the Iran Nuclear Deal has also strained relations.

North Korea:

Reasons: Decades of political and military tensions, including the Korean War, and U.S. policies toward North Korea, such as sanctions, contribute to anti-U.S. sentiments.

Venezuela:

Reasons: Economic sanctions, perceived interference in domestic affairs, and disagreements over governance have fueled anti-U.S. sentiments.

Russia:

Reasons: Historical Cold War tensions, NATO expansion, and geopolitical disagreements contribute to strained U.S.-Russia relations.

China:

Reasons: Trade disputes, geopolitical competition, and differences over issues like Taiwan and the South China Sea contribute to anti-U.S. sentiments.

Cuba:

Reasons: Historical issues, such as the Bay of Pigs invasion and the embargo, have led to longstanding tensions. Recent policy changes have also impacted relations.

Palestinian Territories:

Reasons: The Israeli-Palestinian conflict and U.S. support for Israel contribute to anti-U.S. sentiments in the Palestinian Territories.

Pakistan:

Reasons: Historical U.S. policies, such as support for military regimes, drone strikes, and perceived inconsistencies in the war on terror, contribute to anti-U.S. sentiments.

Afghanistan:

Reasons: Long-term military presence, civilian casualties, and perceived failures in nation-building contribute to negative sentiments.

Iraq:

Reasons: The Iraq War, its aftermath, and the perception of U.S. interference in Iraqi affairs contribute to anti-U.S. sentiments.

It's important to approach these assessments with nuance, recognizing that public opinion can vary within countries and that political contexts can change over time. Public sentiments are complex and can be influenced by a variety of factors, including government policies, historical events, and cultural considerations.

Below are some instances where leaders or individuals from various countries have expressed anti-U.S. sentiments in the past. These instances often reflect political, economic, or cultural tensions and are subject to change over time. Keep in mind that sentiments can evolve, and diplomatic relationships are dynamic.

Iran:

Example: Iranian leaders, including Supreme Leader Ayatollah Ali Khamenei, have frequently criticized U.S. policies, especially concerning the nuclear deal, economic sanctions, and perceived interference in Iranian affairs.

North Korea:

Example: North Korean leader Kim Jong-un has expressed strong anti-U.S. sentiments, often in response to military exercises, sanctions, and perceived threats to the country's sovereignty.

Venezuela:

Example: Former Venezuelan President Hugo Chávez and his successor Nicolás Maduro have criticized U.S. policies, particularly economic sanctions and perceived interference in Venezuelan politics.

Russia:

Example: Russian President Vladimir Putin has, on several occasions, expressed discontent with U.S. actions, including NATO expansion, missile defense systems, and accusations of interference in Russian domestic affairs

China:

Example: Chinese leaders, including President Xi Jinping, have expressed concerns about U.S. policies, such as trade disputes, arms sales to Taiwan, and perceived attempts to contain China's rise as a global power.

Cuba:

Example: Historical animosity between the U.S. and Cuba, dating back to the Cuban Revolution, has led to anti-U.S. sentiments expressed by Cuban leaders, including Fidel Castro and Raúl Castro.

Pakistan:

Example: Various Pakistani leaders have criticized U.S. policies, particularly drone strikes, perceived infringements on Pakistani sovereignty, and fluctuations in aid and military assistance.

Afghanistan:

Example: Afghan leaders have, at times, expressed frustration with U.S. military presence, civilian casualties, and the complexities of the war in Afghanistan.

These examples illustrate instances where leaders from different countries have articulated anti-U.S. sentiments. It's essential to note that political rhetoric is complex, and expressions of sentiment may be influenced by geopolitical dynamics, domestic considerations, and specific policy issues.